W9-BTJ-173

Mornings *with*
Thomas Merton

Mornings *with* Thomas Merton

Readings and Reflections

SELECTED BY

JOHN C. BLATTNER

CHARIS

SERVANT PUBLICATIONS
ANN ARBOR, MICHIGAN

Charis Books is an imprint of Servant Publications especially designed to serve Roman Catholics.

Published by Servant Publications
P.O. Box 8617
Ann Arbor, Michigan 48107

Cover design: Left Coast Design, Portland, OR
Cover photograph: © Catholic News Service. Used by permission.
Interior photographs:
    Pages 23, 48, © Catholic News Service. Used by permission.
    Pages 62, 92, 117, 142 Courtesy of the Thomas Merton Center of Bellarmine College.

    02 03 04 05 06 07 08   10 9 8 7 6 5 4

Printed in the United States of America
ISBN 1-56955-009-3

LIBRARY OF CONGRESS CATALOGING-IN-PUBLICATION DATA

Merton, Thomas, 1915-1968.
    Mornings with Thomas Merton : readings and reflections / selected by John C. Blattner.
        p.   cm.
    Includes bibliographical references.
    ISBN 1-56955-009-3 (alk. paper)
    1. Spiritual life—Catholic Church—Meditations.   I. Blattner, John.   II. Title.
BX2182.2.M39   1998
271'.12502—dc21   97-45998
                                                         CIP

Introduction

Ifirst heard of Thomas Merton in a homily at the student chapel when I was in college. I had recently rediscovered Christianity in the context of the hippie-style "Jesus People" movement of the early 1970s, and was struggling to find some common ground between my newfound fervor and the staid Catholicism of my middle-class Midwestern upbringing.

The homilist had mentioned Merton's name almost in passing, as though there were no question that all his listeners were quite familiar with it. He described Merton as a worldly, intellectual young man who had fallen passionately in love with Christ while a college student, and gone on to become a Trappist monk. I had never heard of Merton. But I was young, and in college, and I fancied myself worldly and intellectual, so I resolved to become better acquainted with this intriguing individual with whom I seemed to have so much in common. I read Merton's autobiography, *The Seven Storey Mountain,* and was both charmed and challenged by the witness of his life, the thoroughness of his conversion, and the profound simplicity of his writing. Ever since, Merton's writings have been an important part of my intellectual and devotional life.

Merton had a long and remarkably varied writing career. He was a prolific literary critic, essayist, poet, biographer, autobiographer, diarist, historian, social commentator, translator, and author of devotional, catechetical, and theological works. A small book like this cannot hope to span such a range of works, nor is it designed to do so. Of necessity, much has been left out. For example, I have decided not to include material from later in Merton's career, such as his scathing commentaries on the modern secular world and his reflections on the relationship between Catholicism and Eastern mysticism—not because they are not good or important, but because they seemed to me to be out of keeping with this book's purpose. My goal has been to bring together samples of Merton's writing that I hope will contribute to the reader's devotional life.

Merton's significance lies as much in who he was as in what he wrote, and the readings in this book focus on how he became the person he was—in particular, how he became the *monk* he was. They focus primarily on selections from *The Seven Storey Mountain;* from Merton's diary of his early years in the monastery, *The Sign of Jonas;* and from his account of the origins of the Trappist order, *The Waters of Siloe*. These are augmented with selections from one of Merton's best-loved devotional works, *No Man Is an Island*.

It is my hope that these selections will serve to introduce (or re-introduce) the reader to one of the most engaging spiritual writers of our time. Most of all, I hope it will help draw the reader closer to Christ, whom Merton loved so passionately.

J.C.B.

1
The Traveler

It is late at night. Most of the Paris cafés have closed their doors and pulled down their shutters and locked them to the sidewalk. Lights are reflected brightly in the wet, empty pavement. A taxi stops to let off a passenger and moves away again, its red tail-light disappearing around the corner.

The man who has just alighted follows a bellboy through the whirling door into the lobby of one of the big Paris hotels. His suitcase is bright with labels that spell out the names of hotels that existed in the big European cities before World War II. But the man is not a tourist. You can see that he is a businessman, and an important one. This is not the kind of hotel that is patronized by mere *voyageurs de commerce*. He is a Frenchman, and he walks through the lobby like a man who is used to stopping at the best hotels. He pauses for a moment, fumbling for some change, and the bellboy goes ahead of him to the elevator.

The traveler is suddenly aware that someone is looking at him. He turns around. It is a woman, and to his astonishment she is dressed in the habit of a nun.

2
The Nun

If he knew anything about the habits worn by the different religious orders, he would recognize the white cloak and brown robe as belonging to the Discalced Carmelites. But what on earth would a man in his position know about Discalced Carmelites? He is far too important and too busy to worry his head about nuns and religious orders—or about churches for that matter, although he occasionally goes to Mass as a matter of form.

The most surprising thing of all is that the nun is smiling, and she is smiling at *him*. She is a young sister, with a bright, intelligent French face, full of the candor of a child, full of good sense; and her smile is a smile of frank, undisguised friendship. The traveler instinctively brings his hand to his hat, then turns away and hastens to the desk, assuring himself that he does not know any nuns. As he is signing the register, he cannot help glancing back over his shoulder. The nun is gone.

Putting down the pen, he asks the clerk, "Who was that nun that just passed by?"

"I beg your pardon, monsieur. What was that you said?"

"That nun—who was she, anyway? The one that just went by and smiled at me."

The clerk arches his eyebrows. "You are mistaken, monsieur. A nun, in a hotel, at this time of night! Nuns don't go wandering around town, smiling at men!"

"I know they don't. That's why I would like you to explain the fact that one came up and smiled at me just now, here in this lobby."

The clerk shrugs: "Monsieur, you are the only person that has come in or gone out in the last half hour."

3
The Monk

Not long after, the traveler who saw that nun in the Paris hotel was no longer an important French industrialist, and he did know something about religious habits. In fact, he was wearing one. It was brown: a brown robe, with a brown scapular over it, and a thick leather belt buckled about the waist. His head was shaven, and he had grown a beard. And he wore a grimy apron to protect his robe from axle grease. He was lying on his back underneath a partly disemboweled tractor. There was a wrench in his hand, and black smudges all around his eyes where he had been wiping the sweat with the back of his greasy hands. He was a lay brother in the most strictly enclosed, the poorest, the most laborious, and one of the most austere orders in the Church.

He had become a Trappist in a southern French abbey. He knew no more of hotels or big cities, because he was living now in the monastery that had been built eight hundred years before by Cistercian monks from Burgundy. And he was living pretty much the way they had lived before him, fasting, praying, reading, keeping silence with his tongue in order that the depths of his mind and heart might be free to seek God—the silent, secret, yet obvious presence of God that is known to the contemplative and unknown to anyone else: not so much because it is unintelligible as because its very excess of intelligibility blinds us and makes us incapable of grasping it. Perhaps the fact that he was working on a tractor instead of on an ox-cart might constitute an accidental difference between him and the monks of the twelfth century; but that is a minor point indeed.

4
The Call

The thing that needs to be stressed about this story is that it is true. That lay brother is living today in the abbey of Aiguebelle, and the reason he is there is to be traced ultimately to the fact that one night he walked into a Paris hotel and saw a nun smiling at him, though the clerk told him no nun was there.

A few days later he saw a picture of the very same nun in the house of some friends. They told him that her name was St. Thérèse of the Child Jesus. Of course he had heard of St. Thérèse. Once more he became interested in the religion he had neglected for so many years. And before long his beard had grown and his head was shaved and he was lying underneath a tractor in a brown robe with axle grease all over his face.

5
The Marine

I do not say that men see apparitions and then run off to become Trappists. It is not necessary to have peculiar experiences before you can become a monk. As a general rule you are better off without experiences. However, there are other experiences, more terrible yet easier to explain—the kind produced by war.

There was a young corporal in the United States Marines who found out at very close quarters what happened to the dead bodies of men left unburied at Okinawa. Then he read a newspaper article about Trappist monks who had started a new monastery in Georgia. When he got out of the Marines, he went home to his family in Wisconsin and told them what was on his mind. They were Catholics, but they did not like the idea of his becoming a Trappist. They told him so with emphasis. His uncle offered him a forty-acre farm, ten head of milk cows, and a team if he would give up his foolish notion. The young man said no.

His mother said, "If you go to that place in Georgia, I will never come to see you."

He went out of the house and started for Georgia.

When he arrived, he found that most of the novices in the new frame monastery of pine planks had also left the armed forces to find a peace that could not exist outside a cloister.

6
Austerity

Life in these monasteries is austere. In fact, when you compare it with the way people live in the world outside, the austerity is fantastic.

Silence. The monks never hold conversations. They use sign language. They talk only to their superiors and to their confessors, which means that they hardly talk at all.

Vigils. They get up in the middle of the night. When they do sleep, they do so not on inner spring mattresses but straw.

Fasting. A shudder goes down the spine of the average American citizen when he learns that the monks never eat fried chicken or apple pie or beefsteak or hot dogs or hamburgers. In fact, they never eat meat. Fish is never served in the common refectory, nor eggs, except to the very old or the very young or the sick. They don't even see milk and cheese for weeks at a time during half the year. They subsist on macaroni or sauerkraut or turnips or spinach or some other unappealing item.

There is no point in multiplying the strange facts of Trappist asceticism without qualifying them, otherwise it will be hard for some people to understand the Trappists. The word "Trappist" has become synonymous with "ascetic" and definitely indicates a monk who leads a very hard life. But unless it is explained just why men lead that life and how they came to do it, there is not much point in simply saying that that is what they do.

Penance and asceticism are not ends in themselves. If monks never succeed in being more than pious athletes, they do not fulfill their purpose in the Church. If you want to understand why the monks lead the life they do, you will have to ask, first of all, What is their aim?

7
The Pursuit of Shadows

If ever there was a country where men loved comfort, pleasure and material security, good health and conversation about the weather and the World Series and the Rose Bowl; if ever there was a land where silence made men nervous and prayer drove them crazy and penance scared them to death, it is America. Yet, quite suddenly, Americans—the healthiest, most normal, most energetic, and most optimistic of the younger generation of Americans—have taken it into their heads to run off to the Trappist monasteries and get their heads shaved and put on robes and scapulars and work in the fields and pray half the night and sleep on straw and, in a word, become monks.

When you ask them why they have done such things, they may give you a very clear answer or, perhaps, only a rather confused answer; but in either case the answer will amount to this: the Trappists are the most austere order they could find, and Trappist life was that which least resembled the life men lead in the towns and cities of our world. And there is something in their hearts that tells them they cannot be happy in an atmosphere where people are looking for nothing but their own pleasure and advantage and comfort and success.

They have not come to the monastery to escape from the realities of life but to find those realities: they have felt the terrible insufficiency of life in a civilization that is entirely dedicated to the pursuit of shadows.

8
Clean Love

What is the use of living for things that you cannot hold on to, values that crumble in your hands as soon as you possess them, pleasures that turn sour before you have begun to taste them, and a peace that is constantly turning into war? Men have not become Trappists merely out of a hope for peace in the next world: something has told them, with unshakable conviction, that the next world begins in this world and that heaven can be theirs now, very truly, even though imperfectly, if they give their lives to the one activity which is the beatitude of heaven.

That activity is love: the clean, unselfish love that does not live on what it gets but on what it gives; a love that increases by pouring itself out for others, that grows by self-sacrifice and becomes mighty by throwing itself away.

9
The Contemplative Life

But there is something very special about the love which is the beatitude of heaven: it makes us resemble God, because God Himself is love. *Deus caritas est.* The more we love Him as He loves us, the more we resemble Him; and the more we resemble Him, the more we come to know Him. And, to complete the circle, the more we know Him, the better we love Him, and "this is eternal life that they may know Thee, the only true God, and Jesus Christ Whom Thou has sent" (Jn 17:3).

That is what is called the contemplative life: a life that is devoted before all else to the knowledge and love of God and to the love of other men in Him and for His sake. It is distinguished, therefore, from the active life, which is directly concerned with the physical and spiritual needs of men first of all. The one main concern of the contemplative is God and the love of God.

10
Purchased with Prayer

Members of the active religious orders take care of the sick and directly feed the poor and teach children in schools. The contemplative monk also contributes indirectly to this work, even in a material way, because the surplus of his farm is given to the poor, and the monastery helps to support hospitals and schools when it is able to do so. So, when the monk works in the fields, he knows he is not merely working for himself; he is working to feed others. But no Trappist monastery can accomplish anything much in the material order. Its greatest work is spiritual. In a world in which men have forgotten the value of prayer, it is the monks who pray for the world and for all those in the world who have forgotten how to pray. If there is some small degree of happiness and spiritual joy and faith to temper the despair of our time, it has been obtained by prayer. And if people have been able to discover any ultimate meaning of the chaos of our world, they owe it to the grace of God, which was obtained for them by somebody's prayer.

11
The Perfection of Love

The monk does not merely exist from day to day, feeding his interior life on the hope of future felicity or the assurance that someone, somewhere, somehow, is profiting by his sacrifice. The substance of the contemplative life is contemplation itself, the possession of God by knowledge and love. That is why contemplation is the perfection of love, the perfection of Christian charity. And for that reason, since "charity is the fulness of the law," contemplation is the perfection of Christianity and the highest form of Christian living. And this is most true when contemplation—that is, the wisdom born of charity—becomes so superabundant that it has to pour itself out and communicate to other men what it knows of God and God's love.

But perfect love for God implies perfect sacrifice. God's love is infinitely selfless and disinterested: what can He possibly gain from the love of His creatures? He seeks our love, not in order that we may give Him something, but because He knows that for us the highest happiness consists in loving Him. But in order to love Him perfectly, we have to love Him with something of the disinterestedness with which He loves us: we have to love Him because He is God.

12
Transforming Union

Love is a union of wills. The perfect love of God is a perfect union of wills with God: that means the inability to will anything that God does not will. In the words of the Cistercian mystic, William of St. Thierry: "Man's perfection is to be like God … in unity of spirit, whereby man not only becomes one with God in the sense that he wills the same things as God, but in the sense that he is *unable to will what God does not will.*" *Non tantum unitate volendi idem, sed aliud velle non valendi.*

This is not something that is arrived at overnight. Nor can any man arrive at it by the practice of virtues that are accessible to his own powers, even aided by ordinary grace. It is a pure gift of God, and it corresponds to what modern mystical theologians call "transforming union."

13
The Eloquence of Silence

Is it any wonder that Trappist monasteries are places full of peace and contentment and joy? These men, who have none of the pleasures of the world, have all the happiness that the world is unable to find. Their silence is more eloquent than all the speeches of politicians and the noise of all the radios in America. Their smiles have more joy in them than has the laughter of thousands. When they raise their eyes to the hills or to the sky, they see a beauty which other people do not know how to find. When they work in the fields and the forests, they seem to be tired and alone, but their hearts are at rest, and they are absorbed in a companionship that is tremendous, because it is three Persons in one infinite Nature, the One Who spoke the universe and draws it all back into Himself by His love; the One from Whom all things came and to Whom all things return: and in Whom are all the beauty and substance and actuality of everything in the world that is real.

14
Hidden Manna

Fed with the hidden manna of contemplation, the monk finds that the words of Ecclesiasticus are realized in his own soul: "With the bread of life and understanding justice shall feed him, and give him the water of wholesome wisdom to drink, and justice shall be made strong in him and he shall not be moved" (Eccl 15:3).

Those who have tasted joy in the silence of the monastery know what the twelfth-century Cistercians meant when they saw the contemplative life in Isaias' symbol of the *"waters of Siloe that flow in silence."*

15
The Monk's Business

A monk is a man who has given up everything in order to possess everything. He is one who has abandoned desire in order to achieve the highest fulfilment of all desire. He has renounced his liberty in order to become free. He goes to war because he has found a kind of war that is peace.

Beyond imagination, beyond grandeur, power, wisdom, and the light of the mind, the monk has found the key to existence in things without romance and without drama—labor, hunger, poverty, solitude, the common life. It is the silence of Christ's Nazareth, in which God is praised without pomp, among the wood shavings.

The monk's business is to empty himself of all that is selfish and turbulent and make way for the unapprehended Spirit of God. That is his ministry and his whole life: to be transformed into God without half realizing, himself, what is going on. Everybody who is drawn to visit the monastery and who can understand what is happening there comes away with the awareness that Christ is living in those men: "That the world may know that Thou hast sent me, and hast loved them as Thou hast also loved me" (Jn 15:22–23).

16
Penance

All contemplative life on earth implies penance as well as prayer, because in contemplation there are always two aspects: the positive one, by which we are united to God in love, and the negative one, by which we are detached and separated from everything that is not God. Without both these elements there is no real contemplation.

17
Community

I f the monk has abandoned the cares and distractions and burdens of life in the world, that does not mean he has renounced
the society of other men or the responsibility of providing for himself by the labor of his own hands: far from it. In giving up his possessions, material ambitions, and independence, the monk dedicates
his whole life, body and soul, to the service of God in his monastic
community. From the moment he makes his vows he gives to God
everything that he has and everything that he is or can be.

18
God Works in Silence

The kings and dictators and the mighty of the world accomplish their works with great noise, with speeches and drums and loud-speakers and brass and the thunder of bombers. But God works in silence.

Nations, dynasties leave their mark upon the world by tearing pieces out of the map, by killing men and sending them into exile or slavery. But while armies destroy with great terror and confusion, God builds life where they have sown death and brings sanctity out of the poisoned stream of their hatred.

19
The Spirit of the World, the Spirit of God

The spirit of the world, which is selfishness and envy and conspiracy and lust and terror, makes men loud from the fear of their own hollowness. But the Spirit of God gives them peace, teaches them not to be afraid of silence but to find themselves in quiet. The spirit of the world, which is avarice and oppression, arms men against one another and divides them against themselves and against others: it splits the world into armed camps. But the Spirit of God draws men together and unites them in peacefulness and teaches them to work together and to carry one another's burdens and to honor one another, in spite of their faults and their weaknesses and their infirmities. It teaches them to be compassionate and to obey one another for the sake of God's love and His peace.

20
Renunciation

The monk becomes poor and gives up the possession of all material things—houses, cars, books, clothes of his own, everything: he even renounces the possession of his own body and his own will. But the only reason why he makes himself poor and struggles to keep himself that way is in order to be immensely rich. For, when he owns nothing, God becomes his fortune, and he owns and enjoys all things in God, his Creator. When the monk ceases to rule and dominate his own life, for the sake of God, it is God Who assumes command of his life and his body and his soul: but to be commanded and ruled entirely by God is to be endowed with His tremendous love, for, whatever God touches, He floods it with the riches of His infinite actuality.

21
Detachment

Even the holiest of things can become possessions when you love them for their own sake. Prayer can become a possession. So can penances. A monk may become just as attached to some little practice of devotion as a manufacturer is to his Packard: and with the same results. He will prefer the pleasure he derives from his private prayers to the good of his brothers and of the community, just as the rich man prefers his own cars and other luxuries to the welfare of the men he employs. A Trappist can be just as attached to some penance as a drunkard is to his bottle, and with the same sort of effect: for he may prefer his penance—which is the choice of his own sweet will—to some real duty, just as the drunkard would rather get drunk than go home and love his family.

22
Means and Ends

There is only one reason for the monk's existence: not farming, not chanting the psalms, not building beautiful monasteries, not wearing a certain kind of costume, not fasting, not manual labor, not reading, not meditation, not vigils in the night, but only GOD.

And that means: love. For God is love. If we love Him we possess Him. Everything else about the monastic life is only a means to that end. When prayer and penance and all the rest cease to be means and become ends in themselves, the contemplative life stops dead and the monk begins to amble along the broad, dreary paths that are trodden by the multitudes of the world.

23
Love Without Limit

But there is one thing in life that has no limit to its value, one virtue that can be practiced without any need for moderation. And that is *love:* the love of God and the love of other men in God and for His sake. *There is no point at which it becomes reasonable to abate your interior love for God or for other men, because that love is an end in itself: it is the thing for which we were created and the only reason why we exist.* Only the exterior acts which are means to this end have to be moderated, because otherwise they would not serve as means and would not bring us to the end. But when the end itself is reached, there is no limit, no need of saying, "It is enough" (see St. Thomas Aquinas, *In Epist. ad Romanus,* xii).

24
Love and Hell

In fact, if you discover any kind of love that satiates you, it is not the end for which you were created. Any act that can cease to be a joy is not the end of your existence. If you grow tired of a love that you thought was the love of God, be persuaded that what you are tired of was never pure love, but either some act ordered to that love or else something without order altogether.

The one love that always grows weary of its object and is never satiated with anything and is always looking for something different and new is the love of ourselves. It is the source of all boredom and all restlessness and all unquiet and all misery and all unhappiness; ultimately, it is hell.

25
Spiritual Blindness

As long as the monk retains private ownership of any corner of his own being, he is that far short of the freedom and purity of love found only in union with the common will. As long as there is any refuge where he can curl up by himself and hug some private good that nobody else is allowed to share, there remains in his heart a cranny in which the dirt of selfishness accumulates. Before he realizes it, he is blinded and stifled by the refuse his subconscious egotism collects. He can no longer see by the light of true faith or breathe the clean air of divine charity, wherein all spiritual health is found.

26
Unity

What a transformation is worked in a community of men by the marvelous power of charity and contemplation, by the power of that pure, disinterested love which is a created participation in the sublime life of God! It turns monasteries into Edens where men can recover the lost innocence of their father Adam. It turns the cloister into a Paradise where the monks begin, even on earth, to imitate the contemplation and praise of the nine choirs of angels—and the angels, remember, are cenobites. One of the greatest joys of monastic life, as of heaven itself, is the consciousness that all this happy contemplation is *shared*. Even if the monk cannot talk or write, and so cannot communicate the joy of his own vision of God to his brethren and to the world, nevertheless the whole atmosphere of the cloister is charged with supernatural happiness and radiant with an indefinable sense of vision which belongs to all: because the whole community is one Contemplative, one Hermit, one Angel, one Seraph in the whole hierarchy of choirs that behold and laud their Creator with tremendous and eternal praises!

27
True Self

After all, what *is* your personal identity? It is what you really are, your real self. None of us is what he thinks he is, or what other people think he is, still less what his passport says he is. Many of us think, no doubt, that we are what we would like to be. And it is fortunate for most of us that we are mistaken. We do not generally know what is good for us.

28
We Are What We Love

We are what we love. If we love God, in Whose images we were created, we discover ourselves in Him and we cannot help being happy: we have already achieved something of the fulness of being for which we were destined in our creation. If we love anything else but God, we contradict the image born in our very essence, and we cannot help being unhappy, because we are a living caricature of what we are meant to be.

29
Prisoner's Base

On the last day of January 1915, under the sign of the Water Bearer, in a year of a great war, and down in the shadow of some French mountains on the borders of Spain, I came into the world. Free by nature, in the image of God, I was nevertheless the prisoner of my own violence and my own selfishness, in the image of the world into which I was born. That world was the picture of hell, full of men like myself, loving God and yet hating Him; born to love Him, living instead in fear and hopeless self-contradictory hungers.

30
Clean Slate

But, oh, how many possibilities there were ahead of me and my brother in that day! A brand-new conscience was just coming into existence as an actual, operating function of a soul. My choices were just about to become responsible. My mind was clean and unformed enough to receive any set of standards, and work with the most perfect of them, and work with grace itself, and God's own values, if I had ever had the chance.

Here was a will, neutral, undirected, a force waiting to be applied, ready to generate tremendous immanent powers of light or darkness, peace or conflict, order or confusion, love or sin. The bias which my will was to acquire from the circumstances of all its acts would eventually be the direction of my whole being towards happiness or misery, life or death, heaven or hell.

More than that: since no man ever can, or could, live by himself and for himself alone, the destinies of thousands of other people were bound to be affected, some remotely, but some very directly and near-at-hand, by my own choices and decisions and desires, as my own life would also be formed and modified according to theirs. I was entering into a moral universe in which I would be related to every other rational being, and in which whole masses of us, as thick as swarming bees, would drag one another along towards some common end of good or evil, peace or war.

31
The Devil Is No Fool

The devil is no fool. He can get people feeling about heaven the way they ought to feel about hell. He can make them fear the means of grace the way they do not fear sin. And he does so, not by light but by obscurity; not by realities but by shadows; not by clarity and substance, but by dreams and the creatures of psychosis. And men are so poor in intellect that a few cold chills down their spine will be enough to keep them from ever finding out the truth about anything.

32
Sacrament

O h, what a thing it is, to live in a place that is so constructed that you are forced, in spite of yourself, to be at least a virtual contemplative! Where all day long your eyes must turn, again and again, to the House that hides the Sacramental Christ!

I did not even know who Christ was, that He was God. I had not the faintest idea that there existed such a thing as the Blessed Sacrament. I thought churches were simply places where people got together and sang a few hymns. And yet now I tell you, you who are now what I once was, unbelievers, it is that Sacrament, and that alone, the Christ living in our midst, and sacrificed by us, and for us and with us, in the clean and perpetual Sacrifice, it is He alone Who holds our world together, and keeps us all from being poured head-long and immediately into the pit of our eternal destruction. And I tell you there is a power that goes forth from that Sacrament, a power of light and truth, even into the hearts of those who have heard nothing of Him and seem to be incapable of belief.

33
Good Fruit

The only really valuable religious and moral training I ever got as a child came to me from my father, not systematically, but here and there and more or less spontaneously, in the course of ordinary conversations. Father never applied himself, of set purpose, to teach me religion. But if something spiritual was on his mind, it came out more or less naturally. And this is the kind of religious teaching, or any other kind of teaching, that has the most effect. "A good man out of the good treasure of his heart, bringeth forth good fruit; and an evil man out of the evil treasure bringeth forth that which is evil. For out of the abundance of the heart the mouth speaketh" (Lk 6:45).

And it is precisely this speech "out of the abundance of the heart" that makes an impression and produces an effect in other people. We give ear and pay at least a partially respectful attention to anyone who is really sincerely convinced of what he is saying, no matter what it is, even if it is opposed to our own ideas.

34
The One Who Suffers Most

Indeed, the truth that many people never understand, until it is too late, is that the more you try to avoid suffering, the more you suffer, because smaller and more insignificant things begin to torture you, in proportion to your fear of being hurt. The one who does most to avoid suffering is, in the end, the one who suffers most: and his suffering comes to him from things so little and so trivial that one can say that it is no longer objective at all. It is his own existence, his own being, that is at once the subject and the source of his pain, and his very existence and consciousness is his greatest torture. This is another of the great perversions by which the devil uses our philosophies to turn our whole nature inside out, and eviscerate all our capacities for good, turning them against ourselves.

35
The Horror of Sin

I was in my room. It was night. The light was on. Suddenly it seemed to me that Father, who had now been dead more than a year, was there with me. The sense of his presence was as vivid and as real and as startling as if he had touched my arm or spoken to me. The whole thing passed in a flash, but in that flash, instantly, I was overwhelmed with a sudden and profound insight into the misery and corruption of my own soul, and I was pierced deeply with a light that made me realize something of the condition I was in, and I was filled with horror at what I saw, and my whole being rose up in revolt against what was within me, and my soul desired escape and liberation and freedom from all this with an intensity and an urgency unlike anything I had ever known before. And now I think for the first time in my whole life I really began to pray—praying not with my lips and with my intellect and my imagination, but praying out of the very roots of my life and of my being, and praying to the God I had never known, to reach down towards me out of His darkness and to help me to get free of the thousand terrible things that held my will in their slavery.

36
The Power of Sin

There has never yet been a bomb invented that is half so power-ful as one mortal sin—and yet there is no positive power in sin, only negation, only annihilation: and perhaps that is why it is so destructive, it is a nothingness, and where it is, there is nothing left—a blank, a moral vacuum.

37
Where Wars Come From

It is only the infinite mercy and love of God that has prevented us from tearing ourselves to pieces and destroying His entire creation long ago. People seem to think that it is in some way a proof that no merciful God exists, if we have so many wars. On the contrary, consider how in spite of centuries of sin and greed and lust and cruelty and hatred and avarice and oppression and injustice, spawned and bred by the free wills of men, the human race can still recover, each time, and can still produce men and women who overcome evil with good, hatred with love, greed with charity, lust and cruelty with sanctity. How could all this be possible without the merciful love of God, pouring out His grace upon us? Can there be any doubt where wars come from and where peace comes from, when the children of this world, excluding God from their peace conferences, only manage to bring about greater and greater wars the more they talk about peace?

We have only to open our eyes and look about us to see what our sins are doing to the world, and have done. But we cannot see. We are the ones to whom it is said by the prophets of God: "Hearing hear, and understand not; and see the vision, and know it not" (Is 6:9).

38
Proclamation

There is not a flower that opens, not a seed that falls into the ground, and not an ear of wheat that nods on the end of its stalk in the wind that does not preach and proclaim the greatness and the mercy of God to the whole world.

There is not an act of kindness or generosity, not an act of sacrifice done, or a word of peace and gentleness spoken, not a child's prayer uttered, that does not sing hymns to God before His throne, and in the eyes of men, and before their faces.

39
Prophets

How does it happen that in the thousands of generations of murderers since Cain, our dark bloodthirsty ancestor, that some of us can still be saints? The quietness and hiddenness and placidity of the truly good people in the world all proclaim the glory of God.

All these things, all creatures, every graceful movement, every ordered act of the human will, all are sent to us as prophets from God. But because of our stubbornness they come to us only to blind us further.

40
The Five Senses

"If any man love the world, the charity of the Father is not in him. For all that is in the world is the concupiscence of the flesh and the concupiscence of the eyes and the pride of life" (1 Jn 2:15–16). That is to say, all men who live only according to their five senses, and seek nothing beyond the gratification of their natural appetites for pleasure and reputation and power, cut themselves off from that charity which is the principle of all spiritual vitality and happiness because it alone saves us from the barren wilderness of our own abominable selfishness.

41
The Limits of Worldliness

It is true that the materialistic society, the so-called culture that has evolved under the tender mercies of capitalism, has produced what seems to be the ultimate limit of this worldliness. And nowhere, except perhaps in the analogous society of pagan Rome, has there ever been such a flowering of cheap and petty and disgusting lusts and vanities as in the world of capitalism, where there is no evil that is not fostered and encouraged for the sake of making money. We live in a society whose whole policy is to excite every nerve in the human body and keep it at the highest pitch of artificial tension, to strain every human desire to the limit and to create as many new desires and synthetic passions as possible, in order to cater to them with the products of our factories and printing presses and movie studios and all the rest.

42
Paradox

There is a paradox that lies in the very heart of human existence. It must be apprehended before any lasting happiness is possible in the soul of a man. The paradox is this: man's nature, by itself, can do little or nothing to settle his most important problems. If we follow nothing but our natures, our own philosophies, our own level of ethics, we will end up in hell.

This would be a depressing thought, if it were not purely abstract. Because in the concrete order of things God gave man a nature that was ordered to a supernatural life. He created man with a soul that was made not to bring itself to perfection in its own order, but to be perfected by Him in an order infinitely beyond the reach of human powers. We were never destined to lead purely natural lives, and therefore we were never destined in God's plan for a purely natural beatitude. Our nature, which is a free gift of God, was given to us to be perfected and enhanced by another free gift that is not due it.

This free gift is "sanctifying grace." It perfects our nature with the gift of life, an intellection, a love, a mode of existence infinitely above its own level. If a man were to arrive even at the abstract pinnacle of natural perfection, God's work would not even be half done: it would be only about to begin, for the real work is the work of grace and the infused virtues and the gifts of the Holy Ghost.

43
God's Life in Us

What is "grace"? It is God's own life, shared by us. God's life is Love. *Deus caritas est.* By grace we are able to share in the infinitely self-less love of Him Who is such pure actuality that He needs nothing and therefore cannot conceivably exploit anything for selfish ends. Indeed, outside of Him there is nothing, and whatever exists, exists by His free gift of its being, so that one of the notions that is absolutely contradictory to the perfection of God is selfishness. It is metaphysically impossible for God to be selfish, because the existence of everything that is depends upon His gift, depends upon His unselfishness.

44
Sanctifying Grace

When a ray of light strikes a crystal, it gives a new quality to the crystal. And when God's infinitely disinterested love plays upon a human soul, the same kind of thing takes place. And that is the life called sanctifying grace.

The soul of man, left to its own natural level, is a potentially lucid crystal left in darkness. It is perfect in its own nature, but it lacks something that it can only receive from outside and above itself. But when the light shines in it, it becomes in a manner transformed into light and seems to lose its nature in the splendor of a higher nature, the nature of the light that is in it.

So that natural goodness of man, his capacity for love which must always be in some sense selfish if it remains in the natural order, becomes transfigured and transformed when the Love of God shines in it.

45
Leading One Another to Christ

Christ established His Church, among other reasons, in order that men might lead one another to Him and in the process sanctify themselves and one another. For in this work it is Christ Who draws us to Himself through the action of our fellow men.

46
"Atheists"

I know that many people are, or call themselves, "atheists" simply because they are repelled and offended by statements about God made in imaginary and metaphorical terms which they are not able to interpret and comprehend. They refuse these concepts of God, not because they despise God, but perhaps because they demand a notion of Him more perfect than they generally find: and because ordinary, figurative concepts of God could not satisfy them, they refuse to listen to philosophy, on the ground that it is nothing but a web of meaningless words spun together for the justification of the same old hopeless falsehoods.

What a relief it was for me, now, to discover not only that no idea of ours, let alone any image, could adequately represent God, but also that we *should not* allow ourselves to be satisfied with any such knowledge of Him.

47
Self-Delusion

I think that if there is one truth that people need to learn, in the world, especially today, it is this: the intellect is only theoretically independent of desire and appetite in ordinary, actual practice. It is constantly being blinded and perverted by the ends and aims of passion, and the evidence it presents to us with such a show of impartiality and objectivity is fraught with interest and propaganda. We have become marvelous at self-delusion; all the more so, because we have gone to such trouble to convince ourselves of our own absolute infallibility. The desires of the flesh—and by that I mean not only sinful desires, but even the ordinary, normal appetites for comfort and ease and human respect, are fruitful sources of every kind of error and misjudgment, and because we have these yearnings in us, our intellects (which, if they operated all alone in a vacuum, would indeed register with pure impartiality what they saw) present to us everything distorted and accommodated to the norms of our desire.

And therefore, even when we are acting with the best of intentions, and imagine that we are doing great good, we may be actually doing tremendous material harm and contradicting all our good intentions. There are ways that seem to men to be good, the end whereof is in the depths of hell.

The only answer to the problem is grace, grace, docility to grace. I was still in the precarious position of being my own guide and my own interpreter of grace. It is a wonder I ever got to the harbor at all!

48
"Take and Read"

I took up the book about Gerard Manley Hopkins. The chapter told of Hopkins at Balliol, at Oxford. He was thinking of becoming a Catholic. He was writing letters to Cardinal Newman (not yet a cardinal) about becoming a Catholic.

All of a sudden, something began to stir within me, something began to push me, to prompt me. It was a movement that spoke like a voice.

"What are you waiting for?" it said. "Why are you sitting here? Why do you still hesitate? You know what you ought to do. Why don't you do it?"

I stirred in the chair, I lit a cigarette, looked out the window at the rain, tried to shut the voice up. "Don't act on impulses," I thought. "This is crazy. This is not rational. Read your book."

Merton with his mother Ruth Jenkins Merton, 1915.

49
"What Are You Waiting For?"

H opkins was writing to Newman, at Birmingham, about his indecision.

"What are you waiting for?" said the voice within me again. "Why are you sitting there? It is useless to hesitate any longer. Why don't you get up and go?"

I got up and walked restlessly around the room. "It's absurd," I thought. "Anyway, Father Ford would not be there at this time of day. I would only be wasting time."

50
"I Want to Be a Catholic"

Suddenly, I could bear it no longer. I put down the book, and got into my raincoat, and started down the stairs. I went out into the street. I crossed over, and walked along by the grey wooden fence, towards Broadway, in the light rain.

And then everything inside me began to sing—to sing with peace, to sing with strength and to sing with conviction.

I had nine blocks to walk. Then I turned the corner of 121st Street, and the brick church and presbytery were before me. I stood in the doorway and rang the bell and waited.

When the maid opened the door, I said: "May I see Father Ford, please?"

"But Father Ford is out."

I thought: well, it is not a waste of time, anyway. And I asked when she expected him back. I would come back later, I thought.

The maid closed the door. I stepped back into the street. And then I saw Father Ford coming down the corner from Broadway. He approached with his head down, in a rapid, thoughtful walk. I went to meet him and said: "Father, may I speak to you about something?"

"Yes," he said, looking up, surprised. "Yes, sure, come into the house."

We sat in the little parlor by the door. And I said: "Father, I want to become a Catholic."

51
Catechism

If people had more appreciation of what it means to be converted from rank, savage paganism, from the spiritual level of a cannibal or of an ancient Roman, to the living faith and to the Church, they would not think of catechism as something trivial or unimportant. Usually the word suggests the matter-of-course instructions that children have to go through before First Communion and Confirmation. Even where it is a matter-of-course, it is one of the most tremendous things in the world, this planting of the word of God in a soul. It takes a conversion to really bring this home.

I was never bored. I never missed an instruction, even when it cost me the sacrifice of some of my old amusements and attractions, which had such a strong hold over me and, while I had been impatient of delay from the moment I had come to that first sudden decision, I now began to burn with desire for Baptism, and to throw out hints and try to determine when I would be received into the Church.

52
Beginning the Climb

As November began, my mind was taken up with this one thought: of getting baptized and entering at last into the supernatural life of the Church. In spite of all my studying and all my reading and all my talking, I was still infinitely poor and wretched in my appreciation of what was about to take place within me. I was about to set foot on the shore at the foot of the high, seven-circled mountain of a Purgatory steeper and more arduous than I was able to imagine, and I was not at all aware of the climbing I was about to have to do.

The essential thing was to begin the climb. Baptism was that beginning, and a most generous one, on the part of God. For, although I was baptized conditionally, I hope that His mercy swallowed up all the guilt and temporal punishment of my twenty-three black years of sin in the waters of the font, and allowed me a new start. But my human nature, my weakness, and the cast of my evil habits still remained to be fought and overcome.

53
My Happy Execution

It was only in the last days before being liberated from my slavery to death, that I had the grace to feel something of my own weakness and helplessness. It was not a very vivid light that was given to me on the subject: but I was really aware, at last, of what a poor and miserable thing I was. On the night of the fifteenth of November, the eve of my Baptism and First Communion, I lay in my bed awake and timorous for fear that something might go wrong the next day. And to humiliate me still further, as I lay there, fear came over me that I might not be able to keep the eucharistic fast. It only meant going from midnight to ten o'clock without drinking any water or taking any food, yet all of a sudden this little act of self-denial which amounts to no more, in reality, than a sort of an abstract token, a gesture of good-will, grew in my imagination until it seemed to be utterly beyond my strength—as if I were about to go without food and drink for ten days, instead of ten hours. I had enough sense left to realize that this was one of those curious psychological reactions with which our nature, not without help from the devil, tries to confuse us and avoid what reason and our will demand of it, and so I forgot about it all and went to sleep.

In the morning, when I got up, having forgotten to ask Father Moore if washing your teeth was against the eucharistic fast or not, I did not wash them, and, facing a similar problem about cigarettes, I resisted the temptation to smoke.

I went downstairs and out into the street to go to my happy execution and rebirth.

54
"Credo!"

The whole thing was very simple. First of all, I knelt at the altar of Our Lady where Father Moore received my abjuration of heresy and schism. Then we went to the baptistery, in a little dark corner by the main door.

I stood at the threshold.

"Quid Petis ab ecclesia Dei?" asked Father Moore.

"Fidem!"

"Fides quid tibi praestat?"

"Vitam aeternam."

Then the young priest began to pray in Latin, looking earnestly and calmly at the page of the *Rituale* through the lenses of his glasses. And I, who was asking for eternal life, stood and watched him, catching a word of the Latin here and there.

He turned to me. *"Abrenuntias Satanae?"*

In a triple vow I renounced Satan and his pomps and his works.

"Dost thou believe in God the Father almighty, Creator of heaven and earth?"

"Credo!"

"Dost thou believe in Jesus Christ His only Son, Who was born, and suffered?"

"Credo!"

"Dost thou believe in the Holy Spirit, in the Holy Catholic Church, the Communion of saints, the remission of sins, the resurrection of the body, and eternal life?"

"Credo!"

55
"Peace Be with Thee"

What mountains were falling from my shoulders! What scales of dark night were peeling off my intellect, to let in the inward vision of God and His truth! But I was absorbed in the liturgy, and waiting for the next ceremony. It had been one of the things that had rather frightened me—or rather, which frightened the legion that had been living in me for twenty-three years.

Now the priest blew into my face. He said: *"Exi ab eo, spiritus immunde:* Depart from him, thou impure spirit, and give place to the Holy Spirit, the Paraclete."

It was the exorcism. I did not see them leaving, but there must have been more than seven of them. I had never been able to count them. Would they ever come back? Would that terrible threat of Christ be fulfilled, that threat about the man whose house was clean and garnished, only to be reoccupied by the first devil and many others worse than himself?

The priest, and Christ in him—for it was Christ that was doing these things through his visible ministry, in the Sacrament of my purification—breathed again in my face. "Thomas, receive the good Spirit through this breathing, and receive the Blessing of God. Peace be with thee."

56
First Communion

Presently the priest's voice was louder, saying the *Pater Noster*. Then, soon, the server was running through the *Confiteor* in a rapid murmur. That was for me. Father Moore turned around and made a big cross in absolution, and held up the little Host.

"Behold the Lamb of God: behold Him Who taketh away the sins of the world."

And my First Communion began to come towards me, down the steps. I was the only one at the altar rail. Heaven was entirely mine—that Heaven in which sharing makes no division or diminution. But this solitariness was a kind of reminder of the singleness with which this Christ, hidden in the small Host, was giving Himself for me, and to me, and, with Himself, the entire Godhead and Trinity—a great new increase of the power and grasp of their indwelling that had begun only a few minutes before at the font.

I left the altar rail and went back to the pew where the others were kneeling like four shadows, four unrealities, and I hid my face in my hands.

57
Temple of God

In the Temple of God that I had just become, the One Eternal and Pure Sacrifice was offered up to the God dwelling in me: the sacrifice of God to God, and me sacrificed together with God, incorporated in His Incarnation. Christ born in me, a new Bethlehem, and sacrificed in me, His new Calvary, and risen in me: offering me to the Father, in Himself, asking the Father, my Father and His, to receive me into His infinite and special love—not the love He has for all things that exist—for mere existence is a token of God's love, but the love of those creatures who are drawn to Him in and with the power of His own love for Himself.

For now I had entered into the everlasting movement of that gravitation which is the very life and spirit of God: God's own gravitation towards the depths of His own infinite nature, His goodness without end. And God, that center Who is everywhere, and whose circumference is nowhere, finding me, through incorporation with Christ, incorporated into this immense and tremendous gravitational movement which is love, which is the Holy Spirit, loved me.

And He called out to me from His own immense depths.

58
Into the Desert

I had come, like the Jews, through the Red Sea of Baptism. I was entering into a desert—a terribly easy and convenient desert, with all the trials tempered to my weakness—where I would have a chance to give God great glory by simply trusting and obeying Him, and walking in the way that was not according to my own nature and my own judgement. And it would lead me to a land I could not imagine or understand. It would be a land that was not like the land of Egypt from which I had come out: the land of human nature blinded and fettered by perversity and sin. It would be a land in which the work of man's hands and man's ingenuity counted for little or nothing: but where God would direct all things, and where I would be expected to act so much and so closely under His guidance that it would be as if He thought with my mind, as if He willed with my will.

It was to this that I was called. It was for this that I had been created. It was for this Christ had died on the Cross, and for this that I was now baptized, and had within me the living Christ, melting me into Himself in the fires of His love.

59
Our Lady

One of the big defects of my spiritual life in that first year was a lack of devotion to the Mother of God. I believed in the truths which the Church teaches about Our Lady, and I said the "Hail Mary" when I prayed, but that is not enough. People do not realize the tremendous power of the Blessed Virgin. They do not know who she is: that it is through her hands all graces come because God has willed that she thus participate in His work for the salvation of men.

To me, in those days, although I believed in her, Our Lady occupied in my life little more than the place of a beautiful myth—for in practice I gave her no more than the kind of attention one gives to a symbol or a thing of poetry. She was the Virgin who stood in the doors of the medieval cathedrals. She was the one I had seen in all the statues in the Musée de Cluny, and whose pictures, for that matter, had decorated the walls of my study at Oakham.

But that is not the place that belongs to Mary in the lives of men. She is the Mother of Christ still, His Mother in our souls. She is the Mother of the supernatural life in us. Sanctity comes to us through her intercession. God has willed that there be no other way.

60
The Inevitability of Sin

I made the terrible mistake of entering upon the Christian life as if it were merely the natural life invested with a kind of supernatural mode by grace. I thought that all I had to do was to continue living as I had lived before, thinking and acting as I did before, with the one exception of avoiding mortal sin.

It never occurred to me that if I continued to live as I had lived before, I would be simply incapable of avoiding mortal sin. For before my Baptism I had lived for myself alone. I had lived for the satisfaction of my own desires and ambitions, for pleasure and comfort and reputation and success. Baptism had brought with it the obligation to reduce all my natural appetites to subordination to God's will.

61
Out of Egypt

It took me time to find it out: but I write down what I have found out at last, so that anyone who is now in the position that I was in then may read it and know what to do to save himself from great peril and unhappiness. And to such a one I would say: Whoever you are, the land to which God has brought you is not like the land of Egypt from which you came out. You can no longer live here as you lived there. Your old life and your former ways are crucified now, and you must not seek to live any more for your own gratification, but give up your own judgement into the hands of a wise director, and sacrifice your pleasures and comforts for the love of God and give the money you no longer spend on those things, to the poor.

Above all, eat your daily Bread without which you cannot live, and come to know Christ Whose Life feeds you in the Host, and He will give you a taste of joys and delights that transcend anything you have ever experienced before, and which will make the transition easy.

62
"A Good Catholic"

Another one of those times that turned out to be historical, as far as my own soul is concerned, was when Lax and I were walking down Sixth Avenue, one night in the spring. The street was all torn up and trenched and banked high with dirt and marked out with red lanterns where they were digging the subway, and we picked our way along the fronts of the dark little stores, going downtown to Greenwich Village. I forget what we were arguing about, but in the end Lax suddenly turned around and asked me the question:

"What do you want to be, anyway?"

I could not say, "I want to be Thomas Merton the well-known writer of all those book reviews in the back pages of the *Times Book Review,*" or "Thomas Merton the assistant instructor of Freshman English at the New Life Social Institute for Progress and Culture," so I put the thing on the spiritual plane, where I knew it belonged, and said:

"I don't know. I guess what I want is to be a good Catholic."

"What do you mean, you want to be a good Catholic?"

The explanation I gave was lame enough, and expressed my confusion, and betrayed how little I had really thought about it at all.

Lax did not accept it. "What you should say"—he told me—"what you should say is that you want to be a saint."

63
"I Want to Be a Saint"

A saint! The thought struck me as a little weird.

I said: "How do you expect me to become a saint?"

"By wanting to," said Lax, simply.

"I can't be a saint," I said, "I can't be a saint." And my mind darkened with a confusion of realities and unrealities: the knowledge of my own sins, and the false humility which makes men say that they cannot do the things that they *must* do, cannot reach the level that they *must* reach: the cowardice that says: "I am satisfied to save my soul, to keep out of mortal sin," but which means by those words: "I do not want to give up my sins and my attachments."

But Lax said: "No. All that is necessary to be a saint is to want to be one. Don't you believe that God will make you what He created you to be, if you will consent to let Him do it? All you have to do is desire it."

A long time ago, St. Thomas Aquinas had said the same thing, and it is something that is obvious to everybody who ever understood the Gospels. After Lax was gone, I thought about it, and it became obvious to me.

The next day I told Mark Van Doren: "Lax is going around saying that all a man needs to be a saint is to want to be one."

"Of course," said Mark.

64
"I Am Going to Be a Priest"

At about one o'clock in the afternoon I went out to get some breakfast, returning with scrambled eggs and toast and coffee in an armful of cardboard containers, different shapes and sizes, and pockets full of new packs of cigarettes. But I did not feel like smoking. We ate and talked, and finally cleared up all the mess and someone had the idea of going for a walk to the Chicken Dock. So we got ready to go.

Somewhere in the midst of all this, an idea had come to me, an idea that was startling enough and momentous enough by itself, but much more astonishing in the context. Perhaps many people will not believe what I am saying.

While we were sitting there on the floor playing records and eating this breakfast, the idea came to me: "I am going to be a priest."

65
Conviction

I cannot say what caused it: it was not a reaction of especially strong disgust at being so tired and so uninterested in this life I was still leading, in spite of its futility. It was not the music, not the fall air, for this conviction that had suddenly been planted in me full grown was not the sick and haunting sort of a thing that an emotional urge always is. It was not a thing of passion or of fancy. It was a strong and sweet and deep and insistent attraction that suddenly made itself felt, but not as movement of appetite towards any sensible good. It was something in the order of conscience, a new and profound and clear sense that this was what I really ought to do.

How long the idea was in my mind before I mentioned it, I cannot say. But presently I said casually: "You know, I think I ought to go and enter a monastery and become a priest."

Gibney had heard that before, and thought I was fooling. The statement aroused no argument or comment, and anyway, it was not one to which Gibney was essentially unsympathetic. As far as he was concerned, any life made sense except that of a businessman. As we went out the door of the house I was thinking: "I am going to be a priest."

66
Crisis

I fixed my eyes on the monstrance, on the white Host.

And then it suddenly became clear to me that my whole life was at a crisis. Far more than I could imagine or understand or conceive was now hanging upon a word—a decision of mine.

I had not shaped my life to this situation: I had not been building up to this. Nothing had been further from my mind. There was, therefore, an added solemnity in the fact that I had been called in here abruptly to answer a question that had been preparing, not in my mind, but in the infinite depths of an eternal Providence.

I did not clearly see it then, but I think now that it might have been something in the nature of a last chance. If I had hesitated or refused at that moment—what would have become of me?

67
"Make Me a Priest"

It was a moment of crisis, yet of interrogation: a moment of searching, but it was a moment of joy. It took me about a minute to collect my thoughts about the grace that had been suddenly planted in my soul, and to adjust the weak eyes of my spirit to its unaccustomed light, and during that moment my whole life remained suspended on the edge of an abyss: but this time, the abyss was an abyss of love and peace, the abyss was God.

It would be in some sense a blind, irrevocable act to throw myself over. But if I failed to do that … I did not even have to turn and look behind me at what I would be leaving. Wasn't I tired enough of all that?

So now the question faced me: "Do you really want to be a priest? If you do, say so...."

The hymn was ending. The priest collected the ends of the humeral veil over his hands that held the base of the monstrance, and slowly lifted it off the altar, and turned to bless the people.

I looked straight at the Host, and I knew, now, Who it was that I was looking at, and I said: "Yes, I want to be a priest, with all my heart I want it. If it is Your will, make me a priest. Make me a priest."

When I had said them, I realized to some measure what I had done with those last four words, what power I had put into motion on my behalf, and what a union had been sealed between me and that power by my decision.

68
Into the Monastery

I was really rather frightened of all religious rules as a whole, and this new step, into the monastery, was not something that presented itself to me, all at once, as something that I would just take in my stride. On the contrary, my mind was full of misgivings about fasting and enclosure and all the long prayers and community life and monastic obedience and poverty, and there were plenty of strange specters dancing about in the doors of my imagination, all ready to come in, if I would let them in. And if I did, how my health would crack up, and my heart would give out, and I would collapse and go to pieces and be cast back into the world a hopeless moral and physical wreck.

All this, of course, was based on the assumption that I was in weak health, for that was something I still believed. Perhaps it was to some extent true, I don't know. But the fear of collapse had done nothing, in the past years, to prevent me from staying up all night and wandering around the city in search of very unhealthy entertainments. Nevertheless, as soon as there was question of a little fasting or going without meat or living within the walls of a monastery, I instantly began to fear death.

69
The Trappists

When Dan began to talk about the one religious Order that filled him with the most enthusiasm, I was able to share his admiration but I had no desire to join it. It was the Order of Cistercians, the Cistercians of the Strict Observance. The very title made me shiver, and so did their commoner name: The Trappists.

70
Spiritual Exercises

It was also at this time that I first attempted any kind of mental prayer. I had bought a copy of the *Spiritual Exercises* of St. Ignatius many months before, and it had remained idle on the shelf.

I had long been a little scared of the *Spiritual Exercises,* having somewhere acquired a false impression that if you did not look out they would plunge you head first into mysticism before you were aware of it. How could I be sure that I would not fly up into the air as soon as I applied my mind to the first meditation? I have since found out that there is very little danger of my ever flying around the premises at mental prayer. The *Spiritual Exercises* are very pedestrian and practical—their chief purpose being to enable all the busy Jesuits to get their minds off their work and back to God with a minimum of wasted time.

I wish I had been able to go through the *Exercises* under the roof of some Jesuit house, directed by one of their priests. However, I went about it under my own direction, studying the rules of procedure that were given in the book, and following them in so far as I managed to grasp what they were all about.

71
The Evil of Sin

There was one theological point that made a very deep impression on me, greater than anything else. Somewhere in the first week, after having considered the malice of mortal sin, I had turned to the evil of venial sin. And there, suddenly, while the horror of mortal sin had remained somewhat abstract to me, simply because there were so many aspects and angles to the question, I clearly saw the malice of venial sin precisely as an offense against the goodness and loving kindness of God, without any respect to punishment. I left that meditation with a deep conviction of the deordination and malice there is in preferring one's own will and satisfaction to the will of God for Whose love we were created.

72
The Humility of Hell

There is a certain kind of humility in hell which is one of the worst things in hell, and which is infinitely far from the humility of the saints, which is peace. The false humility of hell is an unending, burning shame at the inescapable stigma of our sins. The sins of the damned are felt by them as vesture of intolerable insults from which they cannot escape, Nessus shirts that burn them up forever and which they can never throw off.

The anguish of this self-knowledge is inescapable even on earth, as long as there is any self-love left in us: because it is pride that feels the burning of that shame. Only when all pride, all self-love has been consumed in our souls by the love of God, are we delivered from the thing which is the subject of those torments. It is only when we have lost all love of our selves for our own sakes that our past sins cease to give us any cause for suffering or for the anguish of shame.

For the saints, when they remember their sins, do not remember the sins but the mercy of God, and therefore even past evil is turned by them into a present cause of joy and serves to glorify God.

It is the proud that have to be burned and devoured by the horrible humility of hell.... But as long as we are in this life, even that burning anguish can be turned into a grace, and should be a cause of joy.

Merton on his ordination day, May 26, 1949.

73
Heaven's Healing Light

I went to the library one day and took down the *Catholic Encyclopedia* to read about the Trappists.

What I saw on those pages pierced me to the heart like a knife.

What wonderful happiness there was, then, in the world! There were still men on this miserable, noisy, cruel earth, who tasted the marvelous joy of silence and solitude, who dwelt in forgotten mountain cells, in secluded monasteries, where the news and desires and appetites and conflicts of the world no longer reached them.

They were free from the burden of the flesh's tyranny, and their clear vision, clean of the world's smoke and of its bitter sting, were raised to heaven and penetrated into the deeps of heaven's infinite and healing light.

74
The Hidden Men

Outside in the world were holy men who were holy in the sense that they went about with portraits of all the possible situations in which they could show their love of God displayed about them: and they were always conscious of all these possibilities. But these other hidden men had come so close to God in their hiddenness that they no longer saw anyone but Him. They themselves were lost in the picture: there was no comparison between them receiving and God giving, because the distance by which such comparison could be measured had dwindled to nothing. They were in Him. They had dwindled down to nothing and had been transformed into Him by the pure and absolute humility of their hearts.

And the love of Christ overflowing in those clean hearts made them children and made them eternal. Old men with limbs like the roots of trees had the eyes of children and lived, under their grey woolen cowls, eternal. And all of them, the young and the old, were ageless, the little brothers of God, the little children for whom was made the Kingdom of Heaven.

75
"What a Thing Mass Is!"

What a thing Mass becomes, in hands hardened by grueling and sacrificial labor, in poverty and abjection and humiliation! "See, see," said those lights, those shadows in all the chapels. "See Who God is! Realize what this Mass is! See Christ here, on the Cross! See His wounds, see His torn hands, see how the King of Glory is crowned with thorns! Do you know what Love is? Here is Love. Here on this Cross, here is Love, suffering these nails, these thorns, that scourge loaded with lead, smashed to pieces, bleeding to death because of your sins and bleeding to death because of people that will never know Him, and never think of Him and will never remember His Sacrifice. Learn from Him how to love God and how to love men! Learn of this Cross, this Love, how to give your life away to Him."

Almost simultaneously all around the church, at all the various altars, the bells began to ring. These monks, they rang no bells at the *Sanctus* or the *Hanc igitur,* only at the Consecration: and now, suddenly, solemnly, all around the church, Christ was on the Cross, lifted up, drawing all things to Himself, that tremendous Sacrifice tearing hearts from bodies, and drawing them out to Him.

"See, see Who God is, see the glory of God, going up to Him out of this incomprehensible and infinite Sacrifice in which all history begins and ends, all individual lives begin and end, in which every story is told, and finished, and settled for joy or for sorrow: the one point of reference for all the truths that are outside of God, their center, their focus: Love."

"Here Is Love!"

Faint gold fire flashed from the shadowy flanks of the upraised chalice at our altar.

"Do you know what Love is? You have never known the meaning of Love, never, you who have always drawn all things to the center of your own nothingness. Here is Love in this chalice full of Blood, Sacrifice, mactation. Do you not know that to love means to be killed for glory of the Beloved? And where is your love? Where is now your Cross, if you say you want to follow Me, if you pretend you love Me?"

All around the church the bells rang as gentle and fresh as dew.

"But these men are dying for Me. These monks are killing themselves for Me: and for you, for the world, for the people who do not know Me, for the millions that will never know them on this earth...."

78
The Center

The eloquence of this liturgy was even more tremendous: and what it said was one, simple, cogent, tremendous truth: this church, the court of the Queen of Heaven, is the real capital of the country in which we are living. This is the center of all the vitality that is in America. This is the cause and reason why the nation is holding together. These men, hidden in the anonymity of their choir and their white cowls, are doing for their land what no army, no congress, no president could ever do as such: they are winning for it the grace and the protection and the friendship of God.

79
Simplicity

When I saw them at close range, I was amazed at the way these monks, who were evidently just plain young Americans from the factories and colleges and farms and high-schools of the various states, were nevertheless absorbed and transformed in the liturgy. The thing that was most impressive was their absolute simplicity. They were concerned with one thing only: doing the things they had to do, singing what they had to sing, bowing and kneeling and so on when it was prescribed, and doing it as well as they could, without fuss or flourish or display. It was all utterly simple and unvarnished and straightforward, and I don't think I had ever seen anything, anywhere, so unaffected, so unself-conscious as these monks. There was not a shadow of anything that could be called parade or display. They did not seem to realize that they were being watched—and, as a matter of fact, I can say from experience that they did not know it at all.

80
Obscurity

What a strange admission! To say that men were admirable, worthy of honor, perfect, in proportion as they disappeared into a crowd and made themselves unnoticed, by even ceasing to be aware of their own existence and their own acts. Excellence, here, was in proportion to obscurity: the one who was best was the one who was least observed, least distinguished. Only faults and mistakes drew attention to the individual.

The logic of the Cistercian life was, then, the complete opposite to the logic of the world, in which men put themselves forward, so that the most excellent is the one who stands out, the one who is eminent above the rest, who attracts attention.

81
Becoming Real

But what was the answer to this paradox? Simply that the monk in hiding himself from the world becomes not less himself, not less of a person, but more of a person, more truly and perfectly himself: for his personality and individuality are perfected in their true order, the spiritual, interior order, of union with God, the principle of all perfection. *Omnis gloria ejus filiae regis ab intus.*

The logic of worldly success rests on a fallacy: the strange error that our perfection depends on the thoughts and opinions and applause of other men! A weird life it is, indeed, to be living always in somebody else's imagination, as if that were the only place in which one could at last become real!

82
The Fourteenth Station

The Retreat Master, in one of his conferences, told us a long story of a man who had once come to Gethsemani, and who had not been able to make up his mind to become a monk, and had fought and prayed about it for days. Finally, went the story, he had made the Stations of the Cross, and at the final station had prayed fervently to be allowed the grace of dying in the Order.

"You know," said the Retreat Master, "they say that no petition you ask at the fourteenth station is ever refused."

In any case, this man finished his prayer, and went back to his room and in an hour or so he collapsed, and they just had time to receive his request for admission to the Order when he died.

He lies buried in the monks' cemetery, in the oblate's habit.

And so, about the last thing I did before leaving Gethsemani was to do the Stations of the Cross, and to ask, with my heart in my throat, at the fourteenth station, for the grace of a vocation to the Trappists, if it were pleasing to God.

83
Saints

It is a wonderful experience to discover a new saint. For God is greatly magnified and marvelous in each one of His saints: differently in each individual one. There are no two saints alike: but all of them are like God, like Him in a different and special way. In fact, if Adam had never fallen, the whole human race would have been a series of magnificently different and splendid images of God, each one of all the millions of men showing forth His glories and perfections in an astonishing new way, and each one shining with his own particular sanctity, a sanctity destined for him from all eternity as the most complete and unimaginable supernatural perfection of his human personality.

84
"Now Was the Time"

Finally, on the Thursday of that week, in the evening, I suddenly found myself filled with a vivid conviction:

"The time has come for me to go and be a Trappist."

Where had the thought come from? All I knew was that it was suddenly there. And it was something powerful, irresistible, clear.

I picked up a little book called *The Cistercian Life,* which I had bought at Gethsemani, and turned over the pages, as if they had something more to tell me. They seemed to me to be all written in words of flame and fire.

I went to supper, and came back and looked at the book again. My mind was literally full of this conviction. And yet, in the way, stood hesitation: that old business. But now there could be no delaying. I must finish with that, once and for all, and get an answer. I must talk to somebody who would settle it. It could be done in five minutes. And now was the time. Now.

85
"I Want to Give God Everything"

It may seem irrational, but at that moment, it was as if scales fell off my own eyes, and looking back on all my worries and questions, I could see clearly how empty and futile they had been. Yes, it was obvious that I was called to the monastic life: and all my doubts about it had been mostly shadows. Where had they gained such a deceptive appearance of substance and reality? Accident and circumstances had all contributed to exaggerate and distort things in my mind. But now everything was straight again. And already I was full of peace and assurance—the consciousness that everything was right, and that a straight road had opened out, clear and smooth, ahead of me.

Father Philotheus had only one question:

"Are you sure you want to be a *Trappist?*" he asked me.

"Father," I answered, "I want to give God everything."

86
Liberty

I was free. I had recovered my liberty. I belonged to God, not to myself: and to belong to Him is to be free, free of all the anxieties and worries and sorrows that belong to this earth, and the love of the things that are in it. What was the difference between one place and another, one habit and another, if your life belonged to God, and if you placed yourself completely in His hands? The only thing that mattered was the fact of the sacrifice, the essential dedication of one's self, one's will. The rest was only accidental.

"This Time I've Come to Stay"

I rang the bell at the gate. It let fall a dull, unresonant note inside the empty court. My man got in his car and went away. Nobody came. I could hear somebody moving around inside the Gatehouse. I did not ring again. Presently, the window opened, and Brother Matthew looked out between the bars, with his clear eyes and greying beard.

"Hullo, Brother," I said.

He recognized me, glanced at the suitcase, and said: "This time have you come to stay?"

"Yes, Brother, if you'll pray for me," I said.

Brother nodded, and raised his hand to close the window.

"That's what I've been doing," he said, "praying for you."

88
School of Love

The monastery is a school—a school in which we learn from God how to be happy. Our happiness consists in sharing the happiness of God, the perfection of His unlimited freedom, the perfection of His love.

What has to be healed in us is our true nature, made in the likeness of God. What we have to learn is love. The healing and the learning are the same thing, for at the very core of our essence we are constituted in God's likeness by our freedom, and the exercise of that freedom is nothing else but the exercise of disinterested love—the love of God for His own sake, because He is God.

89
The Beginning of Love Is Truth

The beginning of love is truth, and before He will give us His love, God must cleanse our souls of the lies that are in them. And the most effective way of detaching us from ourselves is to make us detest ourselves as we have made ourselves by sin, in order that we may love Him reflected in our souls as He has re-made them by His love.

That is the meaning of the contemplative life, and the sense of all the apparently meaningless little rules and observances and fasts and obediences and penances and humiliations and labors that go to make up the routine of existence in a contemplative monastery: they all serve to remind us of what we are and Who God is—that we may get sick of the sight of ourselves and turn to Him: and in the end, we will find Him in ourselves, in our own purified natures which have become the mirror of His tremendous Goodness and of His endless Love.

90
The First Test

The first and most elementary test of one's call to the religious life—whether as a Jesuit, Franciscan, Cistercian, or Carthusian—is the willingness to accept life in a community in which everybody is more or less imperfect.

The imperfections are much smaller and more trivial than the defects and vices of people outside in the world: and yet somehow you tend to notice them more and feel them more, because they get to be so greatly magnified by the responsibilities and ideals of the religious state, through which you cannot help looking at them.

People even lose their vocations because they find out that a man can spend forty or fifty or sixty years in a monastery and still have a bad temper.

91
Piety and Holiness

It can be said, as a general rule, that the greatest saints are seldom the ones whose piety is most evident in their expression when they are kneeling at prayer, and the holiest men in a monastery are almost never the ones who get that exalted look, on feast days, in the choir. The people who gave up at Our Lady's statue with glistening eyes are very often the ones with the worst temper.

92
Simple Obedience

On one hand there were one or two who exaggerated everything they did and tried to carry out every rule with scrupulousness that was a travesty of the real thing. They were the ones who seemed to be trying to make themselves saints by sheer effort and concentration—as if all the work depended on them, and not even God could help them. But then there were also the ones who did little or nothing to sanctify themselves, as if none of the work depended on them—as if God would come along one day and put a halo on their heads and it would all be over. They followed the others and kept the Rule after a fashion, but as soon as they thought they were sick they started pleading for all the mitigations that they did not already have. And the rest of the time, they fluctuated between a gaiety that was noisy and disquieting, and a sullen exasperation that threw a wet blanket over the whole novitiate.

It was usually the ones that belonged to these two extremes that left and went back to the world. Those who stayed were generally the normal, good-humored, patient, obedient ones who did nothing exceptional and just followed the common rule.

93
Rosary

How sweet it is, out in the fields, at the end of the long summer afternoons! The sun is no longer raging at you, and the woods are beginning to throw long blue shadows over the stubble fields where the golden shocks are standing. The sky is cool, and you can see the pale half-moon smiling over the monastery in the distance.

And you take your rosary out of your pocket, and get in your place in the long file, and start swinging homeward along the road with your boots ringing on the asphalt and deep, deep peace in your heart! And on your lips, silently, over and over again, the name of the Queen of Heaven, the Queen also of this valley: "Hail Mary, full of grace, the Lord is with Thee…." And the Name of her Son, for Whom all this was made in the first place, for Whom all this was planned and intended, for Whom the whole of creation was framed, to be His Kingdom. "Blessed is the fruit of Thy womb, Jesus!"

"Full of grace!" The very thought, over and over, fills our own hearts with more grace: and who knows what grace overflows into the world from that valley, from those rosaries, in the evenings when the monks are swinging home from work!

94
Traveling and Arriving

Before we were born, God knew us. He knew that some of us would rebel against His love and His mercy, and that others would love Him from the moment that they could love anything, and never change that love. He knew that there would be joy in heaven among the angels of His house for the conversion of some of us, and He knew that He would bring us all here to Gethsemani together, one day, for His own purpose, for the praise of His love.

The life of each one in this abbey is part of a mystery. We all add up to something far beyond ourselves. We cannot yet realize what it is. But we know, in the language of our theology, that we are all members of the Mystical Christ, and that we all grow together in Him for Whom all things were created.

In one sense we are always travelling, and travelling as if we did not know where we were going.

In another sense we have already arrived.

We cannot arrive at the perfect possession of God in this life, and that is why we are travelling and in darkness. But we already possess Him by grace, and therefore in that sense we have arrived and are dwelling in the light.

95
The Distance Between Us

Because You have called me here not to wear a label by which I can recognize myself and place myself in some kind of a category. You do not want me to be thinking about what I am, but about what You are. Or rather, You do not even want me to be thinking about anything much: for You would raise me above the level of thought. And if I am always trying to figure out what I am and where I am and why I am, how will that work be done?

I do not make a big drama of this business. I do not say: "You have asked me for everything, and I have renounced all." Because I no longer desire to see anything that implies a distance between You and me: and if I stand back and consider myself and You as if something had passed between us, from me to You, I will inevitably see the gap between us and remember the distance between us.

96
Lost to All Things

That is the only reason why I desire solitude—to be lost to all created things, to die to them and to the knowledge of them, for they remind me of my distance from You. They tell me something about You: that You are far from them, even though You are in them. You have made them and Your presence sustains their being, and they hide You from me. And I would live alone, and out of them. *O beata solitudo!*

For I knew that it was only by leaving them that I could come to You: and that is why I have been so unhappy when You seemed to be condemning me to remain in them. Now my sorrow is over, and my joy is about to begin: the joy that rejoices in the deepest sorrows. For I am beginning to understand. You have taught me, and have consoled me, and I have begun again to hope and learn.

Merton giving a talk to monks at the Abbey of Gethsemani.

97
Last Will and Testament

Yesterday morning I made my will. You always make a will before solemn vows, getting rid of everything, as if you were about to die. It sounds more dramatic than it really is.

98
Our Will, and God's

Trappists believe that everything that costs them is God's will. Anything that makes you suffer is God's will. If it makes you sweat, it is God's will. But we have serious doubts about the things which demand no expense of physical energy. Are they really the will of God? Hardly! They require no steam. We seem to think that God will not be satisfied with a monastery that does not behave in every way like a munitions factory under wartime conditions of production.

If we want something, we easily persuade ourselves that what we want is God's will just as long as it turns out to be difficult to obtain. What is easy is my own will: what is hard is God's will. If I happen to desire something hard to get, it means that I want to sacrifice myself to do God's will. No other standard applies. And because we make fetishes out of difficulties we sometimes work ourselves into the most fantastically stupid situations, and use ourselves up not for God but for ourselves. We think we have done great things because we are worn out. If we have rushed into the fields or into the woods and done a great deal of damage, we are satisfied. We do not mind ruining all our machinery, as long as we make a deafening noise and stir up a great cloud of dust. Something has been achieved.

99
Created for God's Peace

All day I have been waiting for You with my faculties bleeding the poison of unsuppressed activity ... I have waited for Your silence and Your peace to stanch and cleanse them, O my Lord.

You will heal my soul when it pleases You, because I have trusted in You.

I will no longer wound myself with the thoughts and questions that have surrounded me like thorns: that is a penance You do not ask of me.

You have made my soul for Your peace and Your silence, but it is lacerated by the noise of my activity and my desires. My mind is crucified all day by its own hunger for experience, for ideas, for satisfaction. And I do not possess my house in silence.

But I was created for Your peace and You will not despise my longing for the holiness of Your deep silence. O my Lord, You will not leave me forever in this sorrow, because I have trusted in You and I will wait upon Your good pleasure in peace and without complaining any more. This, for Your glory.

100
Mistakes

It seems to me the most absurd thing in the world to be upset because I am weak and distracted and blind and constantly make mistakes! What else do I expect! Does God love me any less because I can't make myself a saint by my own power and in my own way? He loves me more because I am so clumsy and helpless without Him—and underneath what I am He sees me as I will one day be by His pure gift and that pleases Him—and therefore it pleases me and I attend to His great love which is my joy.

101
Perplexity and Growth

God makes us ask ourselves questions most often when He intends to resolve them.

He gives us needs that He alone can satisfy, and awakens capacities that He means to fulfil. Any perplexity is liable to be a spiritual gestation, leading to a new birth and a mystical regeneration.

102
The Simplicity of God

No matter how simple discourse may be, it is never simple enough. No matter how simple thought may be, it is never simple enough. No matter how simple love may be, it is never simple enough. The only thing left is the simplicity of the soul in God, or, better, the simplicity of God.

103
Stumbling and Starting Over

It is not complicated, to lead the spiritual life. But it is difficult. We are blind, and subject to a thousand illusions. We must expect to be making mistakes almost all the time. We must be content to fall repeatedly and to begin again to try to deny ourselves, for the love of God.

It is when we are angry at our own mistakes that we tend most of all to deny ourselves for love of ourselves. We want to shake off the hateful thing that has humbled us. In our rush to escape the humiliation of our own mistakes, we run head first into the opposite error, seeking comfort and compensation. And so we spend our lives running back and forth from one attachment to another.

If that is all our self-denial amounts to, our mistakes will never help us.

The thing to do when you have made a mistake is not to give up doing what you were doing and start something altogether new, but to start over again with the thing you began badly and try, for the love of God, to do it well.

104
Easter

If Mass could only be, every morning, what it is on Easter morning! If the prayers could always be so clear, if the Risen Christ would always shine in my heart and all around me and before me in His Easter simplicity! For His simplicity is our feast, this is the unleavened bread which is manna and the bread of heaven, this Easter cleanness, this freedom, this sincerity. O my God, what can I do to convince You that I long for Your Truth and Your simplicity, to share in Your infinite sincerity which is the mirror of Your True Being, and is Your Second Person! Only the little ones can see Him. He is too simple for any created intelligence to fathom. Sometimes we taste some reflection splashed from the clean Light that is the Life of all things: Baptism; First Mass; Easter Morning. Give us always this bread of heaven. Slake us always with this water that we may not thirst forever.

105
Hope

We can either love God because we hope for something from Him, or we can hope in Him knowing that He loves us. Sometimes we begin with the first kind of hope and grow into the second. In that case, hope and charity work together as close partners, and both rest in God. Then every act of hope may open the door to contemplation, for such hope is its own fulfilment.

Better than hoping for anything from the Lord, besides His love, let us place all our hope in His love itself. This hope is as sure as God Himself. It can never be confounded. It is more than a promise of its own fulfilment. It is an effect of the very love it hopes for. It seeks charity because it has already found charity. It seeks God knowing that it has already been found by Him. It travels to Heaven realizing obscurely that it has already arrived.

106
The Theology of the Father

Jesus is the theology of the Father, revealed to us. Faith tells me that this theology is accessible to all men. Hope tells me that He loves me enough to give Himself to me. If I do not hope in His love for me, I will never really know Christ. I hear of Him by faith. But I do not achieve the contact that knows Him, and thereby knows the Father in Him, until my faith in Him is completed by hope and charity: hope that grasps His love for me and charity that pays Him the return of love I owe.

To consider persons and events and situations only in the light of their effect upon myself is to live on the doorstep of hell. Selfishness is doomed to frustration, centered as it is upon a lie. To live exclusively for myself, I must make all things bend themselves to my will as if I were a god. But this is impossible. Is there any more cogent indication of my creaturehood than the insufficiency of my own will? For I cannot make the universe obey me. I cannot make other people conform to my own whims and fancies. I cannot make even my own body obey me. When I give it pleasure, it deceives my expectation and makes me suffer pain. When I give myself what I conceive to be freedom, I deceive myself and find that I am the prisoner of my own blindness and selfishness and insufficiency.

108
Prayer

As a man is, so he prays. We make ourselves what we are by the way we address God. The man who never prays is one who has tried to run away from himself because he has run away from God. But unreal though he be, he is more real than the man who prays to God with a false and lying heart.

The sinner who is afraid to pray to God, who tries to deny God in his heart, is, perhaps, closer to confessing God than the sinner who stands before God, proud of his sin because he thinks it is a virtue. The former is more honest than he thinks, for he acknowledges the truth of his own state, confesses that he and God are not at peace with one another.

109
Absolute Dependence

All true prayer somehow confesses our absolute dependence on the Lord of life and death. It is, therefore, a deep and vital contact with Him Whom we know not only as Lord but as Father. It is when we pray truly that we really *are*.

110
Music and Silence

We cannot be happy if we expect to live all the time at the highest peak of intensity. Happiness is not a matter of intensity but of balance and order and rhythm and harmony.

Music is pleasing not only because of the sound but because of the silence that is in it: without the alternation of sound and silence there would be no rhythm. If we strive to be happy by filling all the silences of life with sound, productive by turning all life's leisure into work, and real by turning all our being into doing, we will only succeed in producing a hell on earth.

If we have no silence, God is not heard in our music. If we have no rest, God does not bless our work. If we twist our lives out of shape in order to fill every corner of them with action and experience, God will silently withdraw from our hearts and leave us empty.

Let us, therefore, learn to pass from one imperfect activity to another without worrying too much about what we are missing. It is true that we make many mistakes. But the biggest of them all is to be surprised at them: as if we had some hope of never making any.

111
Experience

M istakes are part of our life, and not the least important part. If we are humble, and if we believe in the Providence of God, we will see that our mistakes are not merely a necessary evil, something we must lament and count as lost: they enter into the very structure of our existence. It is by making mistakes that we gain experience, not only for ourselves but for others. And though our experience prevents neither ourselves nor others from making the same mistake many times, the repeated experience still has a positive value.

112
Vocation

Each one of us has some kind of vocation. We are all called by God to share in His life and in His Kingdom. Each one of us is called to a special place in the Kingdom. If we find that place we will be happy. If we do not find it, we can never be completely happy. For each one of us, there is only one thing necessary: to fulfill our own destiny, according to God's will, to be what God wants us to be.

113
Grace to Do the Impossible

In order to be what we are meant to be, we must know Christ, and love Him, and do what He did. Our destiny is in our own hands since God has placed it there, and given us His grace to do the impossible. It remains for us to take up courageously and without hesitation the work He has given us, which is the task of living our own life as Christ would live it in us.

114
Sincerity

We make ourselves real by telling the truth. Man can hardly forget that he needs to know the truth, for the instinct to know is too strong in us to be destroyed. But he can forget how badly he also needs to tell the truth.

115
Truth

We are too much like Pilate. We are always asking, "What is truth?" and then crucifying the truth that stands before our eyes.

What, then, is truth?

Truth, in things, is their reality. In our minds, it is the conformity of our knowledge with the things known. In our words, it is the conformity of our words to what we think. In our conduct, it is the conformity of our acts to what we are supposed to be.

116
Insincerity and Anger

The arguments of religious men are so often insincere, and their insincerity is proportionate to their anger. Why do we get angry about what we believe? Because we do not really believe it. Or else what we pretend to be defending as the "truth" is really our own self-esteem. A man of sincerity is less interested in defending the truth than in stating it clearly, for he thinks that if the truth be clearly seen it can very well take care of itself.

117
Loved by God

If we are to love sincerely, and with simplicity, we must first of all overcome the fear of not being loved. And this cannot be done by forcing ourselves to believe in some illusion, saying that we are loved when we are not. We must somehow strip ourselves of our greatest illusions about ourselves, frankly recognize in how many ways we are unlovable, descend into the depths of our being until we come to the basic reality that is in us, and learn to see that we are lovable after all, in spite of everything!

118
Dying on the Cross

We can only get to Heaven by dying for other people on the cross. And one does not die on a cross by his own unaided efforts. He needs the help of an executioner. We have to die, as Christ died, for those whose sins are to us more bitter than death—most bitter because they are just like our own. We have to die for those whose sins kills us, and who are killed, in spite of our good intentions, by many sins of our own.

If my compassion is true, if it be a deep compassion of the heart and not a legal affair, or a mercy learned from a book and practiced on others like a pious exercise, then my compassion for others is God's mercy for me. My patience with them is His patience with me. My love for them is His love for me.

119
Forgiveness

Do you want to know God? Then learn to understand the weaknesses and imperfections of other men. But how can you understand the weaknesses of others unless you understand your own? And how can you see the meaning of your own limitations until you have received mercy from God, by which you know yourself and Him? It is not sufficient to forgive others: we must forgive them with humility and compassion. If we forgive them without humility, our forgiveness is a mockery: it presupposes that we are better than they. Jesus descended into the abyss of our degradation in order to forgive us after He had, in a sense, become lower than us all. It is not for us to forgive others from lofty thrones, as if we were gods looking down on them from Heaven. We must forgive them in the flames of their own hell, for Christ, by means of our forgiveness, once again descends to extinguish the avenging flame. He cannot do this if we do not forgive others with His own compassion. Christ cannot love without feeling and without heart. His love is human as well as divine, and our charity will be a caricature of His love if it pretends to be divine only, and does not consent to be human.

120
Touched by the Finger of God

If I find Him with great ease, perhaps He is not my God.

If I cannot hope to find Him at all, is He my God?

If I find Him wherever I wish, have I found him?

If He can find me whenever He wishes, and tells me Who He is and who I am, and if I then know that He Whom I could not find has found me: then I know He is the Lord, my God: He has touched me with the finger that made me out of nothing.

Sources

1.   *The Waters of Siloe, xiii*
2.   *The Waters of Siloe, xiii–xiv*
3.   *The Waters of Siloe, xiv–xv*
4.   *The Waters of Siloe, xv*
5.   *The Waters of Siloe, xv–xvi*
6.   *The Waters of Siloe, xvi–xvii*
7.   *The Waters of Siloe, xvii–xviii*
8.   *The Waters of Siloe, xviii*
9.   *The Waters of Siloe, xviii–xix*
10. *The Waters of Siloe, xix*
11. *The Waters of Siloe, xix–xx*
12. *The Waters of Siloe, xx*
13. *The Waters of Siloe, xxi–xxii*
14. *The Waters of Siloe, xxvi–xxvii*
15. *The Waters of Siloe, 3*
16. *The Waters of Siloe, 16*
17. *The Waters of Siloe, 17*
18. *The Waters of Siloe, 332*
19. *The Waters of Siloe, 332*
20. *The Waters of Siloe, 333–34*
21. *The Waters of Siloe, 334–35*
22. *The Waters of Siloe, 335*
23. *The Waters of Siloe, 336*
24. *The Waters of Siloe, 336*
25. *The Waters of Siloe, 342*
26. *The Waters of Siloe, 347*
27. *The Waters of Siloe, 349*
28. *The Waters of Siloe, 349–50*
29. *The Seven Storey Mountain, 3*
30. *The Seven Storey Mountain, 11–12*
31. *The Seven Storey Mountain, 26–27*
32. *The Seven Storey Mountain, 37*
33. *The Seven Storey Mountain, 53–54*
34. *The Seven Storey Mountain, 82–83*
35. *The Seven Storey Mountain, 111*
36. *The Seven Storey Mountain, 128*
37. *The Seven Storey Mountain, 128–29*
38. *The Seven Storey Mountain, 129*
39. *The Seven Storey Mountain, 129*
40. *The Seven Storey Mountain, 133*
41. *The Seven Storey Mountain, 133*
42. *The Seven Storey Mountain, 169*
43. *The Seven Storey Mountain, 169–70*
44. *The Seven Storey Mountain, 170*
45. *The Seven Storey Mountain, 170*
46. *The Seven Storey Mountain, 174–75*
47. *The Seven Storey Mountain, 205–6*
48. *The Seven Storey Mountain, 215*
49. *The Seven Storey Mountain, 215*
50. *The Seven Storey Mountain, 216*
51. *The Seven Storey Mountain, 217*
52. *The Seven Storey Mountain, 221*
53. *The Seven Storey Mountain, 221–22*
54. *The Seven Storey Mountain, 222–23*
55. *The Seven Storey Mountain, 223*
56. *The Seven Storey Mountain, 224*
57. *The Seven Storey Mountain, 224–25*
58. *The Seven Storey Mountain, 226–27*
59. *The Seven Storey Mountain, 229–30*
60. *The Seven Storey Mountain, 230*
61. *The Seven Storey Mountain, 232*
62. *The Seven Storey Mountain, 237–38*

63. *The Seven Storey Mountain*, 238
64. *The Seven Storey Mountain*, 252–53
65. *The Seven Storey Mountain*, 253
66. *The Seven Storey Mountain*, 254–55
67. *The Seven Storey Mountain*, 255
68. *The Seven Storey Mountain*, 262
69. *The Seven Storey Mountain*, 262–63
70. *The Seven Storey Mountain*, 268
71. *The Seven Storey Mountain*, 270
72. *The Seven Storey Mountain*, 295
73. *The Seven Storey Mountain*, 316
74. *The Seven Storey Mountain*, 317
75. *The Seven Storey Mountain*, 323
76. *The Seven Storey Mountain*, 324
77. *The Seven Storey Mountain*, 324
78. *The Seven Storey Mountain*, 325
79. *The Seven Storey Mountain*, 329
80. *The Seven Storey Mountain*, 330
81. *The Seven Storey Mountain*, 330
82. *The Seven Storey Mountain*, 332
83. *The Seven Storey Mountain*, 353
84. *The Seven Storey Mountain*, 363
85. *The Seven Storey Mountain*, 365–66
86. *The Seven Storey Mountain*, 370
87. *The Seven Storey Mountain*, 371
88. *The Seven Storey Mountain*, 372
89. *The Seven Storey Mountain*, 372
90. *The Seven Storey Mountain*, 381
91. *The Seven Storey Mountain*, 382
92. *The Seven Storey Mountain*, 382–83
93. *The Seven Storey Mountain*, 392–93
94. *The Seven Storey Mountain*, 419
95. *The Seven Storey Mountain*, 421
96. *The Seven Storey Mountain*, 421–22
97. *The Sign of Jonas,* 33
98. *The Sign of Jonas,* 49
99. *The Sign of Jonas,* 54
100. *The Sign of Jonas,* 107
101. *The Sign of Jonas,* 186
102. *The Sign of Jonas,* 213
103. *The Sign of Jonas,* 236
104. *The Sign of Jonas,* 290
105. *No Man Is an Island,* 17
106. *No Man Is an Island,* 23
107. *No Man Is an Island,* 24
108. *No Man Is an Island,* 42
109. *No Man Is an Island,* 43
110. *No Man Is an Island,* 127–28
111. *No Man Is an Island,* 128
112. *No Man Is an Island,* 131
113. *No Man Is an Island,* 134–35
114. *No Man Is an Island,* 188
115. *No Man Is an Island,* 189
116. *No Man Is an Island,* 195
117. *No Man Is an Island,* 202
118. *No Man Is an Island,* 212
119. *No Man Is an Island,* 214–15
120. *No Man Is an Island,* 232

Merton, Thomas, *The Waters of Siloe* (Garden City, N.Y.: Garden City Books, 1949).

Merton, Thomas, *The Seven Storey Mountain* (New York, N.Y.: Harcourt, Brace and Company, 1948).

Merton, Thomas, *The Sign of Jonas* (Garden City, N.Y.: Image, 1956).

Merton, Thomas, *No Man Is an Island* (New York, N.Y.: Harcourt, Brace and Company, 1983).